Learn to Read Greek in 5 Days

GEORGIOS PAPADAKIS

ISBN-13: 978-0-9959305-8-2

CONTENTS

Introduction   i

Unit 1 – α, π, κ, μ   1

Unit 2 – ε, τ, β, ρ   3

Unit 3 – ο, ω, λ, σ   5

Unit 4 – ι, η, υ, ν   7

Unit 5 – αι, ει, δ, γ   9

Unit 6 – ου, θ, ζ, φ   11

Unit 7 – αυ, ευ, χ, ξ, ψ   13

Unit 8 – μπ, ντ, γγ   15

Unit 9 – Review   17

Greek Alphabet   19

Glossary – Thematic Order   21

Glossary – Alphabetical Order   29

INTRODUCTION

Learning a new alphabet can be very intimidating for an English speaker only used to reading the Latin alphabet. This is partly why English speakers tend to stick to learning other languages that use the same alphabet, such as French, Spanish and Italian — because they seem a lot easier!

But learning a new alphabet does not have to be so difficult. Many alphabets, including Greek, are probably easier to read than English once you get used to it. The difficulty is finding a good system to learn the new alphabet so that the student does not get discouraged and give up before making any real progress. Making progress in the language is the best motivator.

The secret to learning a new alphabet is to be taught each letter separately, and then to practice how the new letters combine with letters you already know to read real words in the language in a structured way. This is not revolutionary — it is probably how you learned to read English — but it is not easy to find for other languages.

This book will teach you how to read the Greek alphabet in exactly that way, and with this method you will be able to read Modern Greek in only 5 days or less! After that you will be able to enjoy the Greek language and culture in a way that you were never able to before.

THE GREEK ALPHABET
Ελληνικό αλφάβητο

The Modern Greek alphabet contains 24 letters and is written from left to right. The Greek alphabet has been used to write the Greek language since the 8th century BCE. It was originally derived from the Phoenician alphabet, and was the first true alphabet in the world - meaning that it had unique symbols for both consonants and vowels. The Greek alphabet is the ancestor to several other scripts, including the Latin alphabet used to write English, and the Cyrillic alphabet used to write Russian.

The Greek alphabet is not a difficult alphabet to learn for an English speaker, you have probably been exposed to some of the letters already through mathematics or science. Many of the letters look the same or very similar to the Latin letters used for English, especially in their uppercase forms. One of the only difficulties is that some letters look similar to English letters, but are in fact pronounced differently.

Like the Latin alphabet used to write English, the Greek alphabet has both upper and lower case letters. Like in English, uppercase letters are used at the beginning of a sentence and in proper nouns.

This course focuses on the Modern Greek language, as spoken in Greece and Cyprus. The Greek language of the New Testament and the ancient language of classical Athens used the same basic Greek alphabet as the modern language. The older forms of the language do however make use of many more accents and diacritics that are almost completely absent from the modern language.

Although focused on Modern Greek, this book is a great starting point for anyone interested in the older forms of the language. After learning to read Greek with this course, reading ancient Greek would come much easier and is mostly a matter of learning some different accent rules and pronouncing some of the letters differently – the alphabet is the same.

HOW TO USE THIS COURSE

The primary goal of this course book is to teach the reader to recognize the Greek alphabet and to begin to read the Modern Greek language.

The main way this is accomplished is by teaching the individual pronunciations of each letter, and then utilizing "Practice" sections where the student can practice reading real Modern Greek words. These "Practice" sections are very important and the main way the student will start to feel comfortable with the Greek alphabet. The answers to all "Practice" questions are included directly below the questions, but try to avoid looking at the answers until you have attempted to answer the questions yourself.

Throughout the book, the reader will also learn approximately 150 real Modern Greek words. These words have been carefully selected to be of maximum benefit to beginner students of the language and are a great starting point for students who want to continue their study of Greek. In the end of the book there are two glossaries – one in thematic order and one in alphabetical order – where the student can study and memorize all the words learned in this course.

The course material has been designed to be completed slowly over 5 days, while reviewing lessons as necessary. You are encouraged to go at whatever pace you feel comfortable with and to feel free to go back to lessons to review as much as needed.

Good luck and I hope you enjoy the first step on your journey to learning the Greek language.

UNIT 1 - α, π, κ, μ

The first letter introduced in this book is the Greek letter α. This letter is called alfa and like many of the letters in the Greek alphabet, you may have seen it before. The pronunciation of this letter resembles the "a" sound in the English words "spa" and "father" (IPA: /a/). The uppercase form is A.

The letter π is called pi (pronounced "pee" in Greek, not "pie" like in English). π is pronounced like the English "p" in "pear" and "Peter" (IPA: /p/). The uppercase form is Π.

The letter μ, called mi, is pronounced like the English "m" in "mother" or "Mary" (IPA: /m/). The uppercase form is M. Notice how the uppercase form looks more like the English letter than the lowercase form. This is common to many letters in the Greek alphabet.

Try to read the Greek word below:

μαμά

This is the Greek word "mama", which means the same as mama or mommy in English.

The last letter of this unit is the letter κ, called kapa. It is pronounced like the English "k" in "kick" (IPA: /k/). The uppercase form is K.

PRACTICE

Try to recognize these English words in their Greek disguises. The answers are below.

1. μαπ
2. πακ
3. καπ
4. καμπ

ANSWERS

1. map
2. pack
3. cap
4. camp

UNIT 2 - ε, τ, β, ρ

The letter ε, called epsilon, is pronounced like the "e" sound in "dress", or sometimes like the "ay" sound in "play" (IPA: /ε/ or /e/). It will be represented by "e" in this book. The uppercase form is E.

The letter τ, called taf, is pronounced like the "t" sound in "tan" (IPA: /t/). The uppercase form is T.

The letter β is called vita in Modern Greek. Although β resembles an English "B", and historically it was pronounced with a "b" sound, in Modern Greek it is pronounced like the "v" sound in "very" (IPA: /v/). It is important to remember that β is a "v" sound and not a "b" sound when you are reading or speaking in Modern Greek. The uppercase form is B.

The letter ρ, called ro, is pronounced like the "r" sound in Spanish or Italian, that is a trilled or rolled "r" (IPA: /r/). With some practice this is not difficult for English speakers, but until beginner students master it, an English "r" sound may be used. The uppercase form is P. Although ρ resembles an English "p", remember that it is always an "r" sound.

PRACTICE

Try to recognize these English words in their Greek disguises. Focus on the correct pronunciation and not necessarily the English spelling. The answers are below.

1. πετ
2. ταπ
3. βετ

3

4. ραπ
5. κατ
6. ραμ
7. καρ
8. μαρκ
9. παρκ
10. κραμ

ANSWERS

1. pet
2. tap
3. vet
4. rap
5. cat
6. ram
7. car
8. mark
9. park
10. cram

UNIT 3 - ο, ω, λ, σ

The Greek letter ο, called omikron, is pronounced like the "o" sound in "hope" or "rope" (IPA: /o/). The uppercase form is O.

The letter ω, called omega, is also pronounced like the "o" sound in "hope" (IPA /o/). In Modern Greek there is no difference between ο and ω except for the spelling. The uppercase form is Ω.

The letter λ, called lamdha is pronounced like the "l" sound in "lamb" or "like" (IPA: /l/). The uppercase form is Λ.

The letter σ, called sigma, is pronounced like the "s" sound in "sand" (IPA: /s/). The uppercase form is Σ.

When the letter σ is used at the end of a word, a special version of the letter is used, ς. This letter is still pronounced with the same "s" sound, and is the only letter in the Greek alphabet with a different form at the end of a word.

THE ACCENT IN MODERN GREEK

In Modern Greek there is only a single accent in the written language. This is the acute accent and it is written on every word with more than one syllable. The accent looks like this: ά.

The accent tells the reader which syllable the stress falls on; think about the difference between the English words CONduct and conDUCT. Because the stress is always written in Greek, there is no struggle like there is in English in determining which syllable to stress.

5

PRACTICE

Try to read these real Modern Greek words. The English translation is given next to each word. The correct pronunciations are given in the answers below.

1. πατέρας   (father)
2. βάρκα   (boat)
3. πάρκο   (park)
4. πόρτα   (door)
5. άσπρο   (white)
6. σώμα   (body)
7. στόμα   (mouth)
8. καλός   (good)
9. ώρα   (hour)
10. κακός   (bad)

ANSWERS

1. patéras
2. várka
3. párko
4. pórta
5. áspro
6. sóma
7. stóma
8. kalós
9. óra
10. kakós

UNIT 4 - ι, η, υ, ν

The Greek letter ι, called iota, is pronounced like the "ee" sound in "bee" or the "i" in "spaghetti" (IPA: /i/). It will be represented as an "i" throughout this book, but remember to pronounce it like "ee" and not the "i" in "spit". The uppercase form is I.

In Modern Greek, the letter η, called ita, is pronounced exactly the same as ι, i.e. like the "i" in "spaghetti" (IPA: /i/). It will also be represented as "i" in this book. The uppercase form is H, which resembles an uppercase "H" in English, but remember to pronounce it "ee".

The letter υ, called ipsilon, is also pronounced like the "ee" sound in "bee" or the "i" in "spaghetti" (IPA: /i/). This letter will also be represented by "i" in this book to reflect the pronunciation. The uppercase form is Y, which resembles an uppercase "Y" in English.

Although in older forms of Greek the pronunciation of these three letters was distinct, in Modern Greek the difference between ι, η, and υ is merely in the spelling.

The letter ν, called ni, is pronounced like the "n" sound in "no" or "never" (IPA: /n/). Although the Greek letter resembles the English letter "v", remember this letter is pronounced "n" and the letter β is pronounced "v". The uppercase form is N.

DOUBLED CONSONANTS IN MODERN GREEK

In Modern Greek doubled consonants are pronounced the same as if they were written with a single consonant. In older forms of

Greek there was a feature called gemination, meaning consonants that were written twice were held for longer than if the consonant was only written once (Italian still has this feature). This feature has been lost in the modern language, but some words are still written with double consonants. So even though the Modern Greek word for "nine" is written εννέα, it is pronounced [enéa].

PRACTICE

Try to read these Modern Greek words. The English translation is given next to each word. The correct pronunciations are given in the answers below.

1. κορίτσι   (bird)
2. σπίτι   (house)
3. βιβλίο   (book)
4. μύτη   (nose)
5. πόλη   (city)
6. ημέρα   (day)
7. σκύλος   (dog)
8. νερό   (water)
9. τρένο   (train)
10. αεροπλάνο   (airplane)

ANSWERS

1. korítsi
2. spíti
3. vivlío
4. míti
5. póli
6. iméra
7. skílos
8. neró
9. tréno
10. aeropláno

UNIT 5 - αι, ει, δ, γ

In Modern Greek the digraph αι is pronounced as a single letter. It is pronounced like the "e" sound in "dress" or at the end of a word more like the "ay" sound in "play" (IPA: /ε/ or /e/). In Modern Greek αι is pronounced the same as ε. It will be represented as "e" throughout this book to represent the pronunciation.

The digraph ει is pronounced the same as ι, η, and υ (IPA: /i/). It will also be represented as an "i" in this book.

In Modern Greek the letter δ, called dhelta, is pronounced like the "th" sound in "the" or "this" (IPA: /ð/). δ is often written as "d" in English and in older forms of Greek it was pronounced the same as the English "d". Since the pronunciation of this letter in Modern Greek is different, it will be represented in this book as "dh" so that readers are not tempted to pronounce it as the English "d". The uppercase form is Δ.

In Modern Greek the letter γ, called ghama, is pronounced with a sound that does not exist in English. It is like a guttural "g" sound (IPA: /ɣ/). This sound will have to be practiced by listening to a native speaker. γ is often written as "g" in English and in older forms of Greek it was pronounced the same as the English "g". In Modern Greek however, it is pronounced differently and therefore it will be represented by a "gh" in this book. Beginners can think of it as a "g" sound for now but should practice the correct pronunciation.

Before an "e" sound or an "i" sound, γ is pronounced like the "y" sound in "yes" or "yellow" (IPA: /j/), instead of the hard "g" sound it normally has. When this happens it will be represented with a "y" in this book instead of a "gh". The uppercase form of γ is Γ.

PRACTICE

Try to read these Modern Greek words. The English translation is given next to each word. The correct pronunciations are given in the answers below.

1. παιδί   (child)
2. ναι   (yes)
3. τρεις   (three)
4. πόδι   (foot)
5. καρδιά   (heart)
6. δέκα   (ten)
7. οδός   (street)
8. γάλα   (milk)
9. αγόρι   (boy)
10. αγορά   (market)
11. πάγος   (ice)
12. γυναίκα   (woman)
13. γιος   (son)
14. αγελάδα   (cow)

ANSWERS

1. pedhí
2. ne
3. tris
4. pódhi
5. kardhiá
6. dhéka
7. odhós
8. ghála
9. aghóri
10. aghorá
11. pághos
12. yinéka
13. yios
14. ayeládha

UNIT 6 - ου, θ, ζ, φ

The digraph ου is pronounced like the "oo" sound in "boot" or the end of the word "shoe" (IPA: /u/). It will be represented as a "u" in this book.

The letter θ, called thita, is pronounced like the "th" sound in "thigh" or "math" (IPA: /θ/). Note that this is not the same sound as δ, which is pronounced like the "th" sound in "this". δ is a voiced sound, which means the vocal cords vibrate, and θ is voiceless. It will be represented as "th" in this book. The uppercase form is Θ.

The letter ζ, called zita, is pronounced like the "z" sound in "zoo" or "zebra" (IPA: /z/). The uppercase form is Z.

The letter φ, called fi, is pronounced like the "f" sound in "food" or "fun" (IPA: /f/). This letter is often spelled with a "ph" when Greek words are written in English, such as alpha or philosophy. In this book it will be represented as an "f" to represent the pronunciation. The uppercase form is Φ.

PRACTICE

Try to read these Modern Greek words. The English translation is given next to each word. The correct pronunciations are given in the answers below.

1. βουνό   (mountain)
2. ουρανός   (sky)
3. πουλί   (bird)
4. άνθρωπος   (person / man)
5. παράθυρο   (window)

6. θάλασσα	(sea)
7. τραπέζι	(table)
8. μαγαζί	(store / shop)
9. ζεστός	(hot)
10. φωτιά	(fire)
11. καφές	(coffee)
12. κεφάλι	(head)

ANSWERS

1. vunó
2. uranós
3. pulí
4. ánthropos
5. paráthiro
6. thálasa
7. trapézi
8. maghazí
9. zestós
10. fotiá
11. kafés
12. kefáli

UNIT 7 - αυ, ευ, χ, ξ, ψ

The digraph αυ is either pronounced "av" or "af". Before vowels and voiced consonants αυ is pronounced "av". Everywhere else, including at the end of a word, αυ is pronounced "af". This sounds very technical but actually it comes naturally to English speakers as the same process in English turns "wolf" into "wolves".

The digraph ευ is either pronounced "ev" or "ef" based on the same process as αυ.

The letter χ, called khi, is another sound that is not present in English. It is the rough, throat clearing sound in the German "doch" or the "j" in the Spanish "ojos" (IPA: /x/). This letter is often written "ch" but pronounced with a hard "k" sound in English, such as "chronology" or "anarchy". It will be represented as "kh" in this book. The uppercase form is X.

The letter ξ, called ksi, is pronounced the same as the usual pronunciation of the English "x" in words like "vex" or "Texas", i.e. a "k" sound followed by an "s" sound. It will be represented by "ks" in this book. Unlike in English, however, this sound can be used at the beginning of a word and is still pronounced "ks". The uppercase form is Ξ.

The letter ψ, called psi, is pronounced like the "ps" sound in "taps" or "sips", although it is written with one letter in Greek. When this letter is written at the beginning of a word it must still be pronounced as "ps" and not drop the "p" sound like in the English words "psychology" or "pseudo". The uppercase form is Ψ.

PRACTICE

Try to read these Modern Greek words. The English translation is given next to each word. The correct pronunciations are given in the answers below.

1. αυτί	(ear)
2. μαύρος	(black)
3. Παρασκευή	(Friday)
4. Δευτέρα	(Monday)
5. χρόνος	(year)
6. χώρα	(country / state)
7. έξι	(six)
8. ξενοδοχείο	(hotel)
9. ψωμί	(bread)
10. ψάρι	(fish)

ANSWERS

1. aftí
2. mávros
3. paraskeví
4. dheftéra
5. khrónos
6. khóra
7. éksi
8. ksenodhokhío
9. psomí
10. psári

UNIT 8 - μπ, ντ, γγ

The digraph μπ is pronounced "mb" in the middle of words but as a "b" sound at the beginning of words (IPA: /b/).

Similarly, the digraph ντ is pronounced "nd" in the middle of words but as a "d" sound at the beginning of words (IPA: /d/).

The digraph γγ is pronounced like the "ng" sound in "finger" (IPA: /ŋg/). When γ is written before the letters κ, χ, or ξ it is pronounced with the nasal "ng" sound in "singer" (IPA: /ŋ/).

PRACTICE

Try to read these Modern Greek words. The English translation is given next to each word. The correct pronunciations are given in the answers below.

1. μπλε   (blue)
2. μπίρα   (beer)
3. Πέμπτη   (Thursday)
4. δέντρο   (tree)
5. ποντίκι   (mouse)
6. ντολμάς   (dolma, stuffed vine leaves)
7. φεγγάρι   (moon)

ANSWERS

1. ble
2. bíra
3. pémbti
4. dhéndro
5. pondíki
6. dolmás
7. fenghári

UNIT 9 - REVIEW

PRACTICE 1

Review the previous lessons by reading these real Greek place names below. The correct pronunciations are given in the answers below.

1. Αθήνα
2. Πάτρα
3. Θεσσαλονίκη
4. Ηράκλειο
5. Κρήτη
6. Δελφοί
7. Μύκονος
8. Σαντορίνη

ANSWERS 1

1. Athína
2. Pátra
3. Thesaloníki
4. Iráklio
5. Kríti
6. Dhelfí
7. Míkonos
8. Sandoríni

PRACTICE 2

Review what you have learned in this book by reading the Greek names below. The correct pronunciations are given in the Answers below.

1. Παυλόπουλος
2. Παπαδόπουλος
3. Κωνσταντόπουλος
4. Παπαδήμος
5. Θεοδωράκης
6. Παπακώστας

ANSWERS 2

1. Pavlópulos
2. Papadhópulos
3. Konstandópulos
4. Papadhímos
5. Theodhorákis
6. Papakóstas

GREEK ALPHABET

Uppercase	Lowercase	Pronunciation
A	α	[a]
B	β	[v]
Γ	γ	[gh]
Δ	δ	[dh]
E	ε	[e]
Z	ζ	[z]
H	η	[i]
Θ	θ	[th]
I	ι	[i]
K	κ	[k]
Λ	λ	[l]
M	μ	[m]
N	ν	[n]
Ξ	ξ	[ks]
O	o	[o]

Π	π	[p]
P	ρ	[r]
Σ	σ/ς	[s]
T	τ	[t]
Y	υ	[i]
Φ	φ	[f]
X	χ	[kh]
Ψ	ψ	[ps]
Ω	ω	[o]

GLOSSARY – THEMATIC ORDER

ANIMALS

ζώο	[zóo]	animal
σκύλος	[skílos]	dog
γάτα	[gháta]	cat
ψάρι	[psári]	fish
πουλί	[pulí]	bird
αγελάδα	[ayeládha]	cow
γουρούνι	[ghurúni]	pig
ποντίκι	[pondíki]	mouse
άλογο	[álogho]	horse

PEOPLE

άνθρωπος	[ánthropos]	person
μητέρα	[mitéra]	mother
μαμά	[mamá]	mommy / mama
πατέρας	[patéras]	father
μπαμπάς	[bambás]	daddy / papa
γιος	[yios]	son
κόρη	[kóri]	daughter
αδελφός	[adhelfós]	brother
αδελφή	[adhelfí]	sister
φίλος	[fílos]	friend
άνθρωπος	[ánthropos]	man
γυναίκα	[yinéka]	woman
αγόρι	[aghóri]	boy
κορίτσι	[korítsi]	girl
παιδί	[pedhí]	child

TRANSPORTATION

τρένο	[tréno]	train
αεροπλάνο	[aeropláno]	airplane
αυτοκίνητο	[aftokínito]	car (automobile)
ποδήλατο	[podhílato]	bicycle
λεωφορείο	[leoforío]	bus
βάρκα	[várka]	boat

LOCATION

πόλη	[póli]	city
σπίτι	[spíti]	house
οδός	[odhós]	street
αεροδρόμιο	[aerodhrómio]	airport
ξενοδοχείο	[ksenodhokhío]	hotel
εστιατόριο	[estiatório]	restaurant
σχολείο	[scholeío]	school
πανεπιστήμιο	[panepistímio]	university
πάρκο	[párko]	park
μαγαζί	[maghazí]	store / shop
νοσοκομείο	[nosokomío]	hospital
εκκλησία	[eklisía]	church
χώρα	[khóra]	country (state)
τράπεζα	[trápeza]	bank
αγορά	[aghorá]	market

HOME

τραπέζι	[trapézi]	table
καρέκλα	[karékla]	chair
παράθυρο	[paráthiro]	window
πόρτα	[pórta]	door
βιβλίο	[vivlío]	book

CLOTHING

ρούχο	[rúkho]	clothing
καπέλο	[kapélo]	hat
φόρεμα	[fórema]	dress
πουκάμισο	[pukámiso]	shirt
παντελόνι	[pantelóni]	pants
παπούτσι	[papútsi]	shoe

BODY

σώμα	[sóma]	body
κεφάλι	[kefáli]	head
πρόσωπο	[prósopo]	face
τρίχα	[tríkha]	hair
μάτι	[máti]	eye
στόμα	[stóma]	mouth
μύτη	[míti]	nose
αυτί	[aftí]	ear
χέρι	[khéri]	hand / arm
πόδι	[pódhi]	foot / leg
καρδιά	[kardhiá]	heart
αίμα	[éma]	blood

κόκαλο	[kókalo]	bone
γένι	[yéni]	beard

MISCELLANEOUS

ναι	[ne]	yes
όχι	[ókhi]	no

FOOD & DRINK

τροφή	[trofí]	food
κρέας	[kréas]	meat
ψωμί	[psomí]	bread
τυρί	[tirí]	cheese
μήλο	[mílo]	apple
νερό	[neró]	water
μπίρα	[bíra]	beer
κρασί	[krasí]	wine
καφές	[kafés]	coffee
τσάι	[tsái]	tea
γάλα	[ghála]	milk
πρωινό	[proinó]	breakfast
μεσημεριανό	[mesimerianó]	lunch
βραδινό	[vradhinó]	dinner

COLORS

χρώμα	[khróma]	color
κόκκινο	[kókino]	red
μπλε	[ble]	blue
πράσινος	[prásinos]	green

κίτρινος	[kítrinos]	yellow
μαύρος	[mávros]	black
άσπρο	[áspro]	white

NATURE

θάλασσα	[thálasa]	sea
ποτάμι	[potámi]	river
λίμνη	[límni]	lake
βουνό	[vunó]	mountain
βροχή	[vrochí]	rain
χιόνι	[khióni]	snow
δέντρο	[dhéndro]	tree
άνθος	[ánthos]	flower
ήλιος	[ílios]	sun
φεγγάρι	[fenghári]	moon
άνεμος	[ánemos]	wind
ουρανός	[uranós]	sky
φωτιά	[fotiá]	fire
πάγος	[pághos]	ice

ADJECTIVES

μεγάλος	[meghálos]	big
μικρός	[mikrós]	small
καλός	[kalós]	good
κακός	[kakós]	bad
ζεστός	[zestós]	hot
κρύος	[kríos]	cold
φτηνός	[ftinós]	cheap
ακριβός	[akrivós]	expensive

NUMBERS

ένας	[énas]	one
δύο	[dhío]	two
τρεις	[tris]	three
τέσσερις	[téseris]	four
πέντε	[pénde]	five
έξι	[éksi]	six
επτά	[eptá]	seven
οκτώ	[októ]	eight
εννέα	[enéa]	nine
δέκα	[dhéka]	ten

TIME

ημέρα	[iméra]	day
μήνας	[mínas]	month
χρόνος	[khrónos]	year
ώρα	[óra]	hour
σήμερα	[símera]	today
αύριο	[ávrio]	tomorrow
χθες	[khthés]	yesterday

DAYS OF THE WEEK

Κυριακή	[kiriakí]	Sunday
Δευτέρα	[dheftéra]	Monday
Τρίτη	[tríti]	Tuesday
Τετάρτη	[tetárti]	Wednesday
Πέμπτη	[pémbti]	Thursday
Παρασκευή	[paraskeví]	Friday
Σάββατο	[sávato]	Saturday

MONTHS

Ιανουάριος	[ianuários]	January
Φεβρουάριος	[fevruários]	February
Μάρτιος	[mártios]	March
Απρίλιος	[aprílios]	April
Μάιος	[máios]	May
Ιούνιος	[iúnios]	June
Ιούλιος	[iúlios]	July
Αύγουστος	[ávghustos]	August
Σεπτέμβριος	[septémvrios]	September
Οκτώβριος	[októvrios]	October
Νοέμβριος	[noémvrios]	November
Δεκέμβριος	[dhekémvrios]	December

PROPER NAMES

Ελλάδα	[eláda]	Greece
Έλληνας	[élinas]	Greek (person)
ελληνικά	[eliniká]	Greek (language)
Αθήνα	[athína]	Athens

GLOSSARY – ALPHABETICAL ORDER

– A α –

αγελάδα	[ayeládha]	cow
αγορά	[aghorá]	market
αγόρι	[aghóri]	boy
αδελφή	[adhelfí]	sister
αδελφός	[adhelfós]	brother
αεροδρόμιο	[aerodhrómio]	airport
αεροπλάνο	[aeropláno]	airplane
Αθήνα	[athína]	Athens
αίμα	[éma]	blood
ακριβός	[akrivós]	expensive
άλογο	[álogho]	horse
άνεμος	[ánemos]	wind
άνθος	[ánthos]	flower
άνθρωπος	[ánthropos]	person
άνθρωπος	[ánthropos]	man
Απρίλιος	[aprílios]	April
άσπρο	[áspro]	white
Αύγουστος	[ávghustos]	August
αύριο	[ávrio]	tomorrow
αυτί	[aftí]	ear
αυτοκίνητο	[aftokínito]	car (automobile)

– B β –

βάρκα	[várka]	boat
βιβλίο	[vivlío]	book
βουνό	[vunó]	mountain

29

| βραδινό | [vradhinó] | dinner |
| βροχή | [vrokhí] | rain |

– Γ γ –

γάλα	[ghála]	milk
γάτα	[gháta]	cat
γένι	[yéni]	beard
γιος	[yios]	son
γουρούνι	[ghurúni]	pig
γυναίκα	[yinéka]	woman

– Δ δ –

δέκα	[dhéka]	ten
Δεκέμβριος	[dhekémvrios]	December
δέντρο	[dhéndro]	tree
Δευτέρα	[dheftéra]	Monday
δύο	[dhío]	two

– Ε ε –

εκκλησία	[eklisía]	church
Ελλάδα	[eláda]	Greece
Έλληνας	[élinas]	Greek (person)
ελληνικά	[eliniká]	Greek (language)
ένας	[énas]	one
εννέα	[enéa]	nine
έξι	[éksi]	six
επτά	[eptá]	seven
εστιατόριο	[estiatório]	restaurant

– Z ζ –

ζεστός	[zestós]	hot
ζώο	[zóo]	animal

– H η –

ήλιος	[ílios]	sun
ημέρα	[iméra]	day

– Θ θ –

θάλασσα	[thálasa]	sea

– I ι –

Ιανουάριος	[ianuários]	January
Ιούλιος	[iúlios]	July
Ιούνιος	[iúnios]	June

– K κ –

κακός	[kakós]	bad
καλός	[kalós]	good
καπέλο	[kapélo]	hat
καρδιά	[kardhiá]	heart
καρέκλα	[karékla]	chair
καφές	[kafés]	coffee
κεφάλι	[kefáli]	head
κίτρινος	[kítrinos]	yellow

κόκαλο	[kókalo]	bone
κόκκινο	[kókino]	red
κόρη	[kóri]	daughter
κορίτσι	[korítsi]	girl
κρασί	[krasí]	wine
κρέας	[kréas]	meat
κρύος	[kríos]	cold
Κυριακή	[kiriakí]	Sunday

– Λ λ –

| λεωφορείο | [leoforío] | bus |
| λίμνη | [límni] | lake |

– Μ μ –

μαγαζί	[maghazí]	store / shop
Μάιος	[máios]	May
μαμά	[mamá]	mommy / mama
Μάρτιος	[mártios]	March
μάτι	[máti]	eye
μαύρος	[mávros]	black
μεγάλος	[meghálos]	big
μεσημεριανό	[mesimerianó]	lunch
μήλο	[mílo]	apple
μήνας	[mínas]	month
μητέρα	[mitéra]	mother
μικρός	[mikrós]	small
μπαμπάς	[bambás]	daddy / papa
μπίρα	[bíra]	beer
μπλε	[ble]	blue
μύτη	[míti]	nose

– N ν –

ναι	[ne]	yes
νερό	[neró]	water
Νοέμβριος	[noémvrios]	November
νοσοκομείο	[nosokomío]	hospital

– Ξ ξ –

| ξενοδοχείο | [ksenodhokhío] | hotel |

– O o –

οδός	[odhós]	street
οκτώ	[októ]	eight
Οκτώβριος	[októvrios]	October
ουρανός	[uranós]	sky
όχι	[ókhi]	no

– Π π –

πάγος	[pághos]	ice
παιδί	[pedhí]	child
πανεπιστήμιο	[panepistímio]	university
παντελόνι	[pantelóni]	pants
παπούτσι	[papútsi]	shoe
παράθυρο	[paráthiro]	window
Παρασκευή	[paraskeví]	Friday
πάρκο	[párko]	park
πατέρας	[patéras]	father
Πέμπτη	[pémbti]	Thursday

πέντε	[pénde]	five
ποδήλατο	[podhílato]	bicycle
πόδι	[pódhi]	foot / leg
πόλη	[póli]	city
ποντίκι	[pondíki]	mouse
πόρτα	[pórta]	door
ποτάμι	[potámi]	river
πουκάμισο	[pukámiso]	shirt
πουλί	[pulí]	bird
πράσινος	[prásinos]	green
πρόσωπο	[prósopo]	face
πρωινό	[proinó]	breakfast

– P ρ –

| ρούχο | [rúkho] | clothing |

– Σ σ –

Σάββατο	[sávato]	Saturday
Σεπτέμβριος	[septémvrios]	September
σήμερα	[símera]	today
σκύλος	[skílos]	dog
σπίτι	[spíti]	house
στόμα	[stoma]	mouth
σχολείο	[skholío]	school
σώμα	[sóma]	body

– T τ –

τέσσερις	[téseris]	four
Τετάρτη	[tetárti]	Wednesday
τράπεζα	[trápeza]	bank
τραπέζι	[trapézi]	table
τρεις	[tris]	three
τρένο	[tréno]	train
Τρίτη	[tríti]	Tuesday
τρίχα	[tríkha]	hair
τροφή	[trofí]	food
τσάι	[tsái]	tea
τυρί	[tirí]	cheese

– Φ φ –

Φεβρουάριος	[fevruários]	February
φεγγάρι	[fenghári]	moon
φίλος	[fílos]	friend
φόρεμα	[fórema]	dress
φτηνός	[ftinós]	cheap
φωτιά	[fotiá]	fire

– X χ –

χέρι	[khéri]	hand / arm
χθες	[khthés]	yesterday
χιόνι	[khióni]	snow
χρόνος	[khrónos]	year
χρώμα	[khróma]	color
χώρα	[khóra]	country (state)

– Ψ ψ –

ψάρι	[psári]	fish
ψωμί	[psomí]	bread

– Ω ω –

ώρα	[óra]	hour

Other language learning titles available from Wolfedale Press:

Learn to Read Arabic in 5 Days
Learn to Read Armenian in 5 Days
Learn to Read Bulgarian in 5 Days
Learn to Read Georgian in 5 Days
Learn to Read Modern Hebrew in 5 Days
Learn to Read Persian (Farsi) in 5 Days
Learn to Read Russian in 5 Days
Learn to Read Ukrainian in 5 Days

Made in the USA
Coppell, TX
28 April 2022

77190507R00030